Conversational
ITALIAN
for Travelers

Just the Important Phrases
(with Restaurant Vocabulary and Idiomatic Expressions)

Kathryn Occhipinti

Stella *Lucente*

Conversational Italian for Travelers Just the Important Phrases
(with Restaurant Vocabulary and Idiomatic Expressions)
Copyright © October 2022, 4th Edition, by Kathryn Occhipinti

International Standard Book Number: 978-0-9903834-8-2

Publisher: Stella Lucente, LLC
Author: Kathryn Occhipinti
Italian Editors: Simona Giuggioli and Maria Vanessa Colapinto
Graphics and Page Layout: Cyndi Clark
Front Cover Photograph: Piazza San Marco, Venezia
                            Kathryn Occhipinti
Back Cover Photograph: Travel Map of Italy
                          www.map-library.com

Order at:
Internet: www.Learntravelitalian.com **or** www.StellaLucente.com
Stella Lucente, LLC
P.O. Box 9640
Peoria, IL 61612

Table of Contents

The Italian Alphabet

The Italian alphabet has only 21 letters but there are names in Italian for all of the Latin letters, including those traditionally described as foreign to Italian. The letters that are foreign to Italian are listed in parentheses and are included together with the Italian alphabet given below. The written form of each letter's name in Italian and the phonetic pronunciation are listed in separate columns.

Letter	Italian Name	Phonetic Pronunciation	Letter	Italian Name	Phonetic Pronunciation
a	a	ah	q	cu	koo
b	bi	bee	r	èrre	ehr-reh
c	ci	chee	s	èsse	es-seh
d	di	dee	t	ti	tee
e	é	eh	u	u	oo
f	èffe	ehf-feh	v	vu/vi	voo/vee
g	gi	jee	(w)	doppia vu	doh-pee-ah voo
h	àcca	ah-kah	(x)	ics	eeks
i	i	ee	(y)	ipsilon	eep-see-lohn
(j)	i lunga	ee loon-gah		i greca	ee greh-ka
(k)	càppa	kahp-pah	z	zèta	zeh-tah
l	èlle	ehl-leh			
m	èmme	ehm-meh			
n	ènne	ehn-neh			
o	ò	oh			
p	pi	pee			

Conversational Italian for Travelers

The Italian Sound Combinations

Here is the Italian alphabet again, with an example word in Italian to represent how each written letter should sound, as well as an example of an English word that has an equivalent sound. If the sounds are identical in Italian and English, no explanation is given. Multiple examples will be given for a letter if the pronunciation can vary. Italian is one of the most phonetic (and beautiful) languages spoken, and a little time spent learning how to pronounce the letter combinations will make learning the language much easier!

Letters(s)	Italian Pronunciation	English Pronunciation Equivalent	
a	cane	**father**	**ah sound**
b	bene	**bell**	
ca/co/cu	casa	**cat**	**hard c sound**
ci	ciao	**chee**se	**soft ch with long ee sound**
ce	cena	**ch**e**ddar**	**soft ch with short e sound**
chi	chi	**key**	**hard c with long ee sound**
che	che	**kennel**	**hard c with short e sound**
d	dado	**dad**	
e	era	**bet**	**eh sound**
e	vedi	**bait**	**ay sound**
f	farfalla	**fan**	
ga/go/gu	gusto	**good**	**hard g sound**
gi	giro	**jeer**	**soft j with long ee sound**

The Italian Sound Combinations (cont'd)

Letters(s)	Italian Pronunciation	English Pronunciation Equivalent	
ge	gettare	jet	soft j with short e sound
gli	figlio	million	"gli" is a unique Italian sound similar to the "lli" in million, pronounced like mil-lyee-on*
gn	signora	onion	sounds like the letter combination ni in onion
h	--	--	h is not pronounced in Italian
i	vita	meet	long ee sound
l	luna	love	
m	mamma	mother	
n	non	no	
o	sole	soap	oh sound
o	modo	law	aw sound

*To form the sound that corresponds to the letter combination **gli** in Italian, place the tip of your tongue behind your upper teeth. Then, raise the back part of your tongue to the palate and roll your tongue forward to form the guttural "gl" sound that is a part of this combination. Finish with the "yee" sound. By listening, you will note the word **gli** (**the**) stresses the guttural sound, but when the letters **gli** are placed in the middle of a word, such as with **figlio** (**son**), the "yee" part of the **gli** sound is stressed.

The Italian Sound Combinations (cont'd)

Letters(s)	Italian Pronunciation	English Pronunciation Equivalent	
p	pasta	pasta	
qu	quanto	quest	qu together makes the kw sound
r	Roma	---	r is always trilled in Italian
s	rosa	nose	soft s
ss	rossa	toss	hard s
schi	schiavo	skeet	s + chi makes hard skey sound
sche	schema	skill	s + che makes hard skeh sound
sci	sciare	shield	soft sh sound with long ee sound
sce	scemo	shed	soft sh sound with short e sound
t	tu	to	
u	uva	boot	oo sound
v	vincere	vine	
z	zero	zero	soft z
zz	pizza	pizza	hard z, like tz sound

General Pronunciation and Stress
for Italian Words

The Italian language is a phonetic language, so each letter in an Italian word needs to be pronounced to create the final sound. If two vowels are written next to each other, both are pronounced but the sound is a combined sound (referred to as a diphthong). There are many pronunciation rules, but the easiest thing to remember is just to pronounce what you see!

Most Italian words will be stressed on the second to last syllable, which is easy to remember if the word contains only three syllables—just stress the syllable in the middle of the word. In general, a syllable in Italian is usually made up of a vowel or a consonant group with its vowel. The word **ragazzo,** for instance, which means **boy,** will place the stress on the /ga/ sound.

ragazzo   ra/GAZ/zo

There are many exceptions to this rule, however, and the first syllable is stressed instead in many cases for words with three syllables, while the second syllable is often stressed in words with four syllables, as below:

sabato   SA/ba/to
domenica   do/ME/ni/ca

A vowel alone can also form a complete syllable. **Abito (I live),** is a verb with three syllables where the first syllable, which happens to be the vowel /a/, is stressed.

abito   A/bi/to

In the few cases where the very last syllable is stressed, the vowel at the end of the word will be given a grave (`) accent. For example, the Italian word for **city,** which is **città.**

Meeting and Greeting

In Italian, as in English, there are many ways to greet people, and different expressions will be used depending on the situation and how well the individuals know one another. Italian society has become overall less formal. Many easy-going, familiar, and slang expressions are now commonly used, not only between friends and family, but even between acquaintances, although polite forms of address are still important to know.

Listed below are some of the most common ways to greet people. "**Buon giorno**" can be used to mean **"good morning"** or **"hello"** later in the day, when greeting both family members at home and shop owners at the piazza. This phrase can also be used in more formal situations with its literal translation, which is, **"Good day."**

There are at least as many ways to say "good bye" as there are to say "hello," as noted below. Notice that the word ciao is unique, since it can be used as both an informal **"hi"** as well as a quick way to say **"good bye."** Ciao is used frequently throughout Italy today with family and friends.

Buon giorno.*	Good morning. (lit. Good day.)
. . . .	used all day into evening
Buona sera.*	Good evening.
. . . .	early nighttime salutation
Buona notte.*	Good night.
. . . .	used when leaving/at bedtime
Buona giornata.	(Have a) good day.
. . . .	to wish someone a nice (entire) day
Ciao.	Hi. / Bye.
. . . .	informal greeting family/friends

Meeting and Greeting (cont'd)

Salve.	Hello. — both familiar and polite
Ci vediamo!	(Until) we see each other (again)! . . . . for family or for a friend you . . . . hope to see again soon
Arrivederci.	Good bye. . . . . familiar and polite
Arrivederla.	Good bye. . . . . polite, with respect
ArrivederLa.	Good bye. . . . . formal written form
Come va?	How (is it) go(ing)? . . . . a slang greeting used often
Ciao bella!	Hey, beautiful girl!
Ciao bello!	Hey handsome! . . . . for someone you know (well)
A dopo!	(See you) later! . . . . good bye between friends
A più tardi!	(See you) later! . . . . good bye between friends
A presto!	(See you) soon! . . . . good bye between friends

Use these phrases to agree with what someone is saying:

Sì.	Yes.
Certo.	Of course.
D'accordo.	I agree.
Penso di sì.	I think so.
Capisco. / Ho capito.	
	I understand. / I understood.

How to Be Polite in Italian
Piacere, Pregare, Scusarsi **and** Dispiacere

One of the most rewarding aspects of travel is becoming acquainted with the people in the region or country visited. Understanding polite phrases of speech will take one a long way in this regard, as politeness and respect are usually rewarded with the same in return.

There are several very important and helpful verbs of politeness in Italian. The most useful of these verbs is **piacere,** with the meaning of **to like/to be pleasing to,** from which one of the phrases for "please" is derived.

The Italian word **favore** translates into the English word **favor.** The two different ways to say **please** in Italian, **per piacere** and **per favore,** are interchangeable, and loosely translate into **"for a pleasantry/nicety"** or **"for a favor."**

Grazie is a noun that means **thanks,** and used in the same way as the English phrase **"thank you."** If you are really pleased, say, **"Molte grazie!" "Tante grazie!"** or **"Mille grazie!"** Or, use the most popular form, **"Grazie mille!"**

Per favore. / Per piacere.	**Please.**
Grazie.	Thank you.
Molte grazie!	Thank you very much!
Tante grazie!	Thank you so much!
Mille grazie! / Grazie mille!	Thanks a lot! (lit. A thousand thanks!)

*Can be written as one word, as in **buongiorno, buonasera,** or **buonanotte.**

How to Be Polite in Italian (cont'd)
Piacere, Pregare, Scusarsi and Dispiacere

"**Prego!**" is the direct response to "**Grazie,**" and means, "**You're welcome!**" It is derived from another verb of politeness, **pregare,** which has several meanings. **Pregare** can be translated as **to pray,** which lends itself to the connotation of asking or requesting something.

English phrases like, "I pray of you," "I beg of you," or "Pray tell," carry the same idea, although these are no longer commonly used. In a similar way, a simple, "**Prego...**" can also be used with a gesture to address someone when on line in a crowded place, with the meaning, "**Go ahead of me, I beg you.**"

"**Sono pregati di...**" is a polite expression derived from **pregare** that may also be heard when someone in charge, such as a flight attendant or a tour guide, is directing a group of people.

Finally, if a waiter comes to the table with a wonderful dish for you to try, he may put this in front of you with a flourish and say, "**Prego!**" as in, "**Here you go!**"

Prego!	You're welcome!
Prego...	If (you) please...
. . . .	can be used if you would like a stranger to go ahead of you in a line, usually with a gesture.
Prego!	Here you go!
Sono pregati di...	Are requested/asked/begged to...
. . . .	polite phrase used with a group
Di niente.	It was nothing. / You're welcome.

How to Be Polite in Italian (cont'd)
Piacere, Pregare, Scusarsi and Dispiacere

Scusarsi means **to excuse oneself,** and is used frequently in crowded situations in its polite command form, **"Mi scusi."** **"Scusa"** is the form used between people who know one another.

Dispiacere is a verb that is used to convey the ideas of **sadness, sorrow,** and **regret** and so, **"Mi dispiace,"** means, **"I'm sorry."**

Another expression that is useful when navigating an unfamiliar place, and especially when entering an unfamiliar building is, **"Permesso?"** This expression comes from the shortened form of the phrase, **"Permesso di entrata?"** The literal meaning is, **"Permission to enter?"** and the shortened form of this question, **"Permesso?"** is useful in situations when in English we would ask, **"May I come in?"**

Here are some essential phrases to get one through the throngs of tourists in Italy:

Mi scusi.	Excuse me. (polite command)
Scusa.	Excuse me. (familiar command)
Mi dispiace.	I'm sorry.
Permesso?	Permission to enter?
	May I come in?

When addressing someone as **you,** Italians use the familiar **tu** and the polite, or formal, **Lei.** Some formal titles:

Signore	Mister / Sir
Signora	Misses / Madam / Ma'am
Signorina	Miss

Basic Communication

For the dialogues that are a part of the **Conversational Italian for Travelers** series of books,* Caterina speaks simple, basic Italian. Here are some simple phrases that may help in real life situations, when it may be difficult to understand exactly what is said during a conversation in Italian. Also, notice that Italians do not insert the word "do" at the beginning of their questions, as is proper in English.

Most Italians have some knowledge of English, and will try to oblige by speaking in both Italian and English if needed, choosing the words they know best from each language. Don't be afraid to use a few Italian phrases yourself when conversing in Italy. Somehow, it all works out in the end!

If you are asked,

Parla italiano?	(Do) you speak Italian?

You may reply,

Si, un po'.	Yes, a little.
Si, molto bene.	Yes, very well.
No, mi dispiace!	No, I am sorry!
Parla inglese?	(Do) you speak English?

An Italian may say,

Si, capisco inglese.	Yes, I understand English.
No, parlo soltanto italiano.	No, I only speak Italian.
Dov'è un interprete?	Where is an interpreter?

*To listen to the audio dialogues for the story **Caterina Travels to Italy,** visit the website www.learntravelitalian.com or Amazon.com.

If you are having difficulty understanding fluent Italian, you may want to say:

Che cosa?	What?
Non capisco.	I don't understand.

Non capisco che cosa hai detto.
    I don't understand what you said.

Non ho sentito.	I didn't hear (you).

Lei parla troppo veloce (per me)!
    You speak too fast (for me)!

Per favore, può...	Please, could you...
...parlare più lentamente?	...speak more slowly?
...parlare più piano?	...speak more slowly/softly?
...parlare più forte?	...speak more loudly?
...parlare in inglese?	...speak in English?

Non parlare troppo veloce.	Don't speak too quickly.
Può ripetere?	Could you (pol.) repeat (that)?

Come si dice...?
    How (do) you say...? (lit. How does one say...?)
Come si dice in italiano?
    How (do) you say it in Italian?

Cosa significa?	What does it mean?
Come si chiama quello?	What is that called?

Just the Important Phrases   15

Common Expressions: Here it is!
Dove and Ecco

Many Italian expressions do not make sense if each word is translated literally, but only together do the words form a commonly understood message. These types of phrases can be called "idiomatic expressions." Note that many of the "common expressions" in the meeting/greeting section are "idiomatic" and just need to be memorized.

On the other hand, a single Italian word may take the place of an entire phrase in English. Let's look at the answers to the interrogative expressions for **where is/where are** (**dov'è** and **dove sono**).

The typical answer of **here/there is/are** is **ecco. Ecco** is a single word in Italian that encompasses both the adverbs **here/there** and the verbs **is/are.** Note that **ecco** is typically used to point out something that is in plain sight.

Below are common expressions used to describe where something or someone is.

Dove?	Where?
Dov'è...?	Where is...?
Dove sono...?	Where are...?
Ecco...	Here is... / Here are... There is... / There are...
Eccolo! / Eccola!	Here he is! / Here she is! / Here it is!
Eccomi!	Here I am!

Grammar Note
Describing Where You Are From

One of the most frequently asked questions during polite conversation is, "Where are you from?" Two phrases can be used to ask this question in Italian.

The first phrase uses the combination:

di + dove + essere	of + where + to be

This phrase is used to inquire about an individual's place of birth, with the understanding that this is often the same town the person is still living in. In Italian, when the verb **to be** (**essere**) is used with **di** (**of**), as in, "Of where are you?" this implies, "Where do you belong?" In proper English, of course, we would say, "Where are you from?" Although the Italian sentence structure sounds awkward in English, the rule in Italian is never to end a sentence with a preposition.

The answer in Italian will also use **essere** with **di** and will be followed by the town of one's birth. Notice that the subject pronoun **io** (**I**) is usually left out of the answer, as it is understood from the conjugation of the verb **essere.**

Di dov'è Lei?	Where are you (pol.) from?
Di dove sei?	Where are you (fam.) from?
Sono di Chicago.	I am from Chicago.

The second phrase uses the combination:

da + dove + venire	from + where + to come

Grammar Note
Describing Where You Are From (cont'd)

This phrase uses the action verb **venire** and may come up in conversation when someone is visiting Italy or has moved to a new place. One can simply state their nationality. Alternatively, the reply can use the **io** form of **venire**, which is **vengo,** and **da** for **from,** followed by a city, town, region/state, or country.

Also, remember that when speaking in Italian about a region, state, or country, the Italian definite article (**the**) (**il, la, l', gli**) must be included. The preposition **da** is then combined with the definite article to make **dal, dallo, dall', dalla,** or **dagli,** which all mean **"from the."** The subject pronoun is omitted in Italian, as usual, and so is given in parentheses in the English translations below. For now, don't worry about these rules. Just look up and remember the correct way to say where you are living in case you are asked!

Da dove viene? / Da dove vieni?
    Where do you come from? (pol.)/(fam.)

Sono americano(a). / Sono italo-americano(a).
    (I) am American. / (I) am Italian-American.

Vengo dagli Stati Uniti.
    (I) come from (am from) the United States.

Vengo dall'Illinois.
    (I) come from Illinois.

Vengo dalla California.
    (I) come from California.

Vengo dal New Jersey.
    (I) come from New Jersey.

Vengo da Chicago.
    (I) come from Chicago.

Common Expressions—"How old are you?"
"Quanti anni hai?"

The question of one's age comes up often in conversation—even when traveling—when documents are checked or new friends are made for instance. In English, we say, **"How old <u>are</u> you?"** using the verb **to be,** as a statement of fact. But, Italians look at this question as the number of years accumulated during a lifetime (and maybe the wisdom accumulated during those years?) so they use the verb **to have,** which is **avere.** The common Italian expressions regarding age are really just another way of looking at things!

The familiar way to ask the question in Italian is, **"Quanti anni hai?"** or literally, **"How many years do you have?"**

Quanti anni hai?   How old are you?
(lit. How many years do you have?)

After this question is asked of you, the response will also use the verb **avere,** and you will respond:

(Io)* Ho _____ anni. I have _____ years.

It is not necessarily considered bad manners for someone to lie about their age (depending on the situation)! But, whatever age one chooses to give, there are a couple of rules that are used to make conversation flow more easily in Italian.

1. The tens (20, 30, 40, etc.) drop their last vowel _before the word anni_. In this case, the expression would be:

Ho vent'anni.   I have 20 years.

Ho trent'anni.   I have 30 years.

Ho quarant'anni.   I have 40 years.

Common Expressions—"How old are you?"
"Quanti anni hai?" (cont'd)

2. All numbers that end in **uno** (21, 31, 41, etc), drop the final
   –o _before a noun that starts with a vowel_.

So, if one is 21, 31, or 41 years old, the reply would be as
follows:

Ho ventun'anni.	I have 21 years.
Ho trentun'anni.	I have 31 years.
Ho quarantun'anni.	I have 41 years.

No need to remember these rules—for now, just look up and
commit to memory your age and the ages of your immediate
family members!

One more thing, after all these rules—suppose the speakers are
discussing the age of someone else? In this case, the question
and answer (using the third person singular) would be:

Quanti anni ha (una persona)?

How old is (a person)?
(lit. How many years does (a person) have?)

Lui/Lei ha _____ anni.

He/She has _____ years.

*The subject pronoun **io** is used in the first example sentence but
is usually omitted in conversation.

To complete our discussion of age, here is a general list of terms that refer to us as we grow from a baby to an adult and also to the family members that we interact with.

il bambino/bimbo	baby (male)
la bambina/bimba	baby (female)
il ragazzino	little boy
la ragazzina	little girl
il ragazzo	boy / young man
la ragazza	girl / young woman
l'uomo	man
il signore / il marito	gentleman / husband
la donna	woman
la signora / la moglie	lady / married woman / wife
la signorina	young lady (unmarried)
il padre / papà	father / dad
la madre / mamma	mother / mom
il figlio / la figlia / i figli	son / daughter / children
il cugino / la cugina	cousin (male/female)

Opera fans may recall two operas with somewhat antiquated words used to describe a girl in the title: *La Fanciulla del West (The Pretty Young Girl of the West)* by Giacomo Puccini and *La Gioconda (The Merry Girl)* by Amilcare Ponchielli. La Gioconda is also the Italian name for the Mona Lisa.

Grammar Note
Italian Street Addresses

In Italy, the format for street addresses is different from that in the United States. The word **via** for **street** <u>precedes</u> the Italian street name and is not capitalized when written. The number of the building is given <u>after</u> the street name and is followed by the apartment number.

The Italian abbreviation **int.** stands for **interno,** and is used instead of a number sign before the apartment number. Writing the apartment number of the address is not always necessary in Italy though, as in many towns families have lived in the same house for generations!

The second line of the address gives the **Italian zip code** for the city (**Codice Avviamento Postale,** or **CAP**) and then the name of the city. The **CAP** should always be included. The region may be written in parentheses after the city as well and is usually abbreviated.

Here is our character Caterina's (fictional) address* in proper English and then converted into the Italian format:

6 North Michigan Street, #22
via North Michigan, 6 int. 22

Chicago, IL 61615 USA
61615 Chicago (IL), USA

The real-life example below is the address for the US Embassy in Rome:

Ambasciata degli Stati Uniti d'America a Roma
via Vittorio Veneto, 121
00187 Roma (RM), Italia

*From **Caterina Travels to Italy,** www.learntravelitalian.com and Amazon.com.

Grammar Note
Saying the Date in Italian

Here is the way to say the date in Italian:

> **definite article** + **number** + **di** + **month**

This is actually a lot easier than it may look! Below are a few examples. You will notice that in English we say, "January second," for "January 2," while in Italian the phrasing and word order reads: "the two of January." The exception to this rule is the first day of the month. In this case, the Italian ordinal number **primo,** which means **first,** must always be used, instead of **uno** (**one**). Also, the months and days of the week are not capitalized when written in Italian.*

Oggi è il due di gennaio.
    Today is January 2.

Domani è il tre di gennaio.
    Tomorrow is January 3.

Dopodomani è il quattro di gennaio.
    The day after tomorrow is January 4.

Oggi è il primo di agosto.
    Today is August 1st.

To say, "On Mondays..." referring to something that happens every Monday, just use the definite article **il** (**the**) at the beginning of the sentence for all the masculine weekdays ending in **ì**. Use **la** for the feminine **Sunday** (**domenica**).

Il lunedì vado al lavoro. / La domenica vado in chiesa.
    On Mondays, I go to work.
    On Sundays, I go to church.

*When writing the date, remember the order of the day and the month are reversed in Italy (as in Europe): dd/mm/yyyy.

Money

The word **euro** is invariable in Italian—the ending is the same whether we are speaking of one or one million **euros!** Also, although in English we pronounce the word "euro" something like "your/ro," the Italian word is pronounced with the Italian **u**, which has an "oo" sound. Phonetically, the Italian word **euro** is pronounced something like this: "ehoo/ro," with one syllable running directly into the next.

Here are some important phrases to use when changing money:

Dov'è una banca?   Where is a bank?

Cerco un bancomat.
    I am looking (for) an ATM machine.

Ho bisogno di cambiare i soldi.
    I need to change money.

Vorrei cambiare i soldi.
    I would like to change money.

Ho bisogno di cambiare i dollari con l'euro.
    I need to change (the money in) dollars for
    (the money in) euros.

Vorrei cambiare i dollari con l'euro.
    I would like to change dollars for euros.

Qual è il tasso di cambio?
    What is the exchange rate?

Qual è la tariffa?
    What is the fee (for exchanging)?

Qual è la percentuale?
    What is the percent?

It may also be helpful to know some phrases that can be used to negotiate with the local merchants in the **piazza.**

We begin by asking:

Quanto costa...	How much is...
	(lit. How much costs...)

Of course, the listed price may be:

troppo caro	too expensive
costoso	expensive/costly
proprio costoso	really expensive
Costa un occhio della testa!	
	Costs an arm and a leg!
	(lit. Costs an eye out of the head!)

Unless the article happens to be:

in vendita	on sale
in saldo / saldi	on sale for a reduced price
in svendita	in a closeout sale
sconto / scontato	discount / discounted
a prezzo basso	at a low or lowered price

Money (cont'd)

Once we have decided on that perfect souvenir, here are the different methods to use to pay for it!

If you want to ask if a certain method of payment is accepted, you could say:

Posso/Può pagare con...	Can I/Can you pay with...
...la carta di credito?	...a credit card?*
...il bancomat?	...a debit card?*
...in contanti?	...in cash?
...un assegno?*	...a check?**

And the answer will usually be:

Accettiamo la carta di credito.	
	We accept credit card(s).
Accettiamo il bancomat.	We accept debit card(s).
Non accettiamo assegni.*	We do not accept checks.**
Documento, per favore...	Identification, please...

* Notice the Italian use of the definite articles **il** and **la** for these phrases, while in American conversation the convention is to use **a.**

**Italian checks are not usually accepted for small purchases, and foreign checks are not likely to be accepted at all!

To ask for the check in a restaurant, simply say:

Il conto, per favore.   The check, please.

When dining, a service charge may be included and should be listed on the restaurant bill—always look at the bill or ask your waiter if you are not sure. It is usually called the **coperto** (**cover**) or the **pane e coperto** (**bread and cover**), as there is always a charge of at least 1.5 or 2.0 euros for the bread served before a meal in Italy.

In tourist areas, a **service charge** (**servizio**) of 10-20% may be added onto the bill. Italians will generally not eat in a restaurant with this additional service charge, although tourists usually don't seem to notice or mind this charge.

Both the **coperto** and the **servizio** should also be listed in the menu, though, as required by law in Italy.

A little more is sometimes left for the waiter as a tip as well, but this does not have to be a certain percentage of the bill and is usually determined by "rounding up" the payment by a few euros to make it easier to pay in cash.

È incluso il servizio?   Is the service charge included?

Tenga il resto.   Keep the change.

If you only have large bills or if you want a receipt, you might ask:

Mi può portare il resto, per favore?
    Could you (pol.) bring me the change, please?

Mi può dare la ricevuta, per favore?
    Could you (pol.) give me a receipt, please?

Vocabulary
At the Train Station

This vocabulary list may be helpful for navigating the typical Italian train station and train routes. You may want to try the automatic ticket machines if there is a long line at the ticket counter or order online at www.trenitalia.com.

TRANSPORTATION

il binario	train track/train rail
la fermata	the stop (along a train or bus route)
la prima fermata	the first stop
la prossima fermata	the next stop
l'ultima fermata	the last stop

locale/regionale
  local train which makes all stops of the route

diretto
  direct/non-stop train to the stated destination

espresso
  express/non-stop train to the stated destination

intercity
  train which goes from one major city to another

la macchina obliteratrice
  ticket canceling and date validating stamping
  machine (green or yellow box on a wall by the tracks)

il sottopassaggio/sottopasso
  underpass used to get to train tracks at a station

cambio treno	change train(s)
la coincidenza	the connection

　　Conversational Italian for Travelers

l'andata	the journey there
	the act of leaving on a trip
il ritorno	the return trip
	the act of coming back
l'andata e ritorno	round trip (leave and return)
il biglietto di sola andata	one way ticket
il biglietto di andata e ritorno	round trip ticket
il supplemento	additional charge
l'ora	hour
l'orario	schedule
l'arrivo	arrival
la partenza	departure
la valigia	suitcase
il bagaglio	baggage
il deposito bagagli	luggage check room
il bagagliaio	luggage compartment
la carrozza	train car
lo scompartimento	compartment in a train
il posto / i posti	seat / seats
occupato(a) / riservato(a)	
occupied (seat) / reserved (seat)	
libero(a)	free, open (seat)

Buying a Ticket and Taking the Train

Here is a summary of important phrases travelers need to know to get around town on public transportation. Notice that Italians say they need or want a ticket **for,** with the word **per,** rather than the more usual English **to.** Also, although one could use the word **voglio,** for **"I want,"** it is considered more polite to instead use **vorrei,** which means, **"I would like."**

Vorrei un biglietto per Milano.
   I would like a ticket for Milan.

Vorrei un biglietto di andata e ritorno.
   I would like a round trip ticket.
   (lit. a ticket of going and returning)

Voglio prendere il treno diretto.
   I want to take the direct train (non-stop train).

Devo pagare il supplemento?
   Must (I) pay an extra fee (for fast trains)?

Vorrei il locale.
   I would like the local (many stops on the route).

Cambio/Cambi treno a...
   I/You change train(s) at...

Non vorrei cambiare treno.
   I don't want to change train(s).

Devo cambiare treno?
   Must I change train(s)?

Quanto ci vuole per la coincidenza?
   How much time (is needed) for the connection?

Dov'è l'orario?   Where is the (train) schedule?

A che ora parte il treno?
    At what time (does) the train leave?

A che ora arriva il treno?
    At what time (does) the train arrive?

Prendo il treno per Milano alle dieci.
    I take the train for Milan at 10 AM.

È questo il treno per Milano?
    Is this the train for Milan?

È questa la fermata per Milano?
    Is this the stop for Milan?

È la prossima fermata per Milano?
    Is the next stop for Milan?

Sta per partire.	**It's about to leave.**
Sta partendo.	**It's leaving (right now).**
Sta arrivando.	**It's arriving (right now).**

Il treno sta arrivando/sta partendo.
    The train is arriving/departing (right now).

Hai perso il treno!	**You (fam.) have missed the train!**
Ho perso il treno!	**I have missed the train!**

Ho preso il treno sbagliato!
    I have taken the wrong train!

Asking for Assistance

While visiting an unfamiliar city, it may be necessary to ask a stranger for help. An easy way to politely phrase any question you have is to use the phrase, **"Mi può..."** which means, **"Could you (polite)... me."** Then, simply _add the infinitive verb for what you need at the end of the Italian phrase—there is no need to conjugate using this method!_ If we add **dire** to the phrase, for instance, we get, **"Mi può dire..."** for **"Could you (polite) tell me..."**

The polite form of the verb **sapere** (**to know a fact**), **sa,** can also be used in many situations to ask if someone knows the information you need with the phrase, **"Lei sa..."**

Mi scusi...	Excuse me (pol. command)...
Mi può...?	Could you (pol.)... me...?
Lei sa...?	(Do) you (pol.) know...?

You can put together many sentences asking the location of a place as follows:

Mi scusi, <u>mi può dire</u> dov'è...
    Excuse me, <u>could you (pol.) tell me</u> where is...

Mi scusi, <u>Lei sa</u> dov'è...
    Excuse me, <u>(do) you (pol.) know</u> where is...

...l'albergo?	...the hotel?
...il ristorante?	...the restaurant?
...la banca?	...the bank?
...la metro/metropolitana?	...the subway?
...la fermata dell'autobus?	...the bus stop?
...la stazione dei treni?	...the train station?

Use a similar format to ask questions about schedules:

Mi scusi, <u>mi può dire</u> quando...
    Excuse me, <u>could you (pol.) tell me</u> when...

Mi scusi, <u>Lei sa</u> quando...
    Excuse me, <u>(do) you (pol.) know</u> when...

...arriva il treno?	...the train arrives? (lit. arrives the train)
...arriva l'autobus?	...the bus arrives?
...parte il treno?	...the train leaves? (lit. leaves the train)
...parte l'autobus?	...the bus leaves?
...apre il museo?	...the museum opens? (lit. opens the museum)
...chiude il museo?	...the museum closes?

If the answer to these questions involves a particular street, the answer you will hear will use the phrase **in... via** for the English **on... street.**

La banca è <u>in via</u> Verde. The bank is <u>on</u> Green <u>Street</u>.

Helpful expressions for those driving:

Può controllare l'olio / le gomme / l'acqua?
    Could you check the oil / the tires / the water?

Può cambiare la gomma? Could you change the tire?

Può fare il pieno?   Could you fill it up?

Il pieno, per favore!   Fill it up, please!

Vocabulary
Driving in the City and on the Highway

il paese	town / village
la città	city
il centro	downtown
la piazza	town square
il palazzo	large building (inhabited)
l'edificio	large building (exterior)
la strada / la via	road / street / way
la calle	Venetian for narrow street
il vicolo	narrow street / alley
l'automobilista	driver
il traffico	traffic
il semaforo	traffic light
il cartello (stradale)	(road) sign
il senso unico	one-way street
il senso vietato	forbidden street / no entry
l'angolo	corner
l'incrocio	intersection
il marciapiede	sidewalk
l'area pedonale	pedestrian zone
l'autostrada	superhighway
la tangenziale	peripheral road / bypass

l'entrata	(highway) entrance
l'uscita	(highway) exit
la deviazione	detour
il limite di velocità	speed limit
vietato	forbidden / no entry
la corsia	lane
il sorpasso	overtake / pass
la corsia di sorpasso	passing lane
la corsia di emergenza	emergency lane / shoulder
la corsia a scorrimento veloce	express lane
la scorciatoia	shortcut
l'autogrill	rest stop with food
il parcheggio	parking lot / parking space
il disco orario	parking disc / timer
porta via	tow away
il carro attrezzi	tow truck
il carrabile	driveway
passo carrabile	no parking driveway

il divieto di sosta
    no parking / forbidden stopping

il divieto di accesso
    no access / no trespassing / forbidden entry

Renting a Car—Take me?/Get in!

Autonoleggio	Car rental
Quanto costa?	How much does it cost?
Quanto costa al giorno?	What does it cost for the day?

Quanto costa alla settimana?
   What does it cost for a week?

Che modelli avete?	What models do you have?
Mi mostri, per favore!	Show me, please! (pol. command)
È tutto compreso?	Is everything included?

È compresa l'assicurazione?
   Is the insurance included?

È compresa la benzina?	Is the gas included?
C'è l'imposta IVA?	Is there a value added tax?

If you would like a ride from a taxi or help from a friend to get somewhere, begin with **"Mi può..."** or **"Vorrei..."**

Mi può chiamare un tassì, per favore?
   Could you (pol.) call me a taxi, please?

Mi può portare...
   Could you (pol.) take me... (as in drive me)

Vorrei prendere il treno.   I want to take the train.

C'è una stazione della metro vicino?
   Is there a subway station/stop near-by?

Note that different prepositions are used for cars vs. other forms of transportation when *getting in*. Also, the prepositions **su** (**on**) and **da** (**from/out of**) are combined with the different forms of **the** (**il, l', or la**).

To help you understand the Italian sentence structure, the prepositions are given in red and the combined prepositions underlined. The verbs are in green and the nouns in blue.

Salgo in macchina.   I get into the car.

Salgo su...   I get on/I board/I go aboard...

Salgo... sull'autobus, sul treno, sulla motocicletta, sulla bicicletta, sull'areo.
> I get onto... the bus, the train, the motorcycle, the bicycle, the airplane.

Scendo da...   I go down/I get down/I get off or out of...

Scendo dalla macchina.   I get out of the car.

Scendo... dall'autobus, dal treno, dalla motocicletta, dalla bicicletta, dall'areo.
> I get off of... the bus, the train, the motorcycle, the bicycle, the airplane.

Sali in macchina!   Get into the car!
                                 (fam. command)

Scendi dalla macchina!   Get out of the car!
                                 (fam. command)

Dammi le chiavi (della macchina)!
> Give me the (car) keys! (fam. command)

Just the Important Phrases   37

Coming and Going

The verb **andare** is an irregular Italian verb that means **to go.** The verb that means **to go out, uscire,** and the verb that means **to come, venire,** are both also irregular. Remember the phrase, **"Vengo dall'America,"** which means, **"I come from America"?** We will now use the verb **venire,** along with **uscire,** for some of our important phrases.

Here are some simple phrases of coming and going that may be useful for the traveler. **"Vieni qua!"** for instance, which means, **"Come here!"** is a helpful phrase for the family trying to stay together.

Also helpful to remember is, **"Vengo io,"** a phrase used to emphasize one's intention to do something right away, as in, *"I* am **(the one who is)** coming **(to take care of it)."** Use this phrase when other people are in the room and you are the one volunteering to answer the door.

The "you familiar" form is used for the following example phrases. Notice the insertion of the preposition **a,** for **to,** *after* the conjugated forms of **andare** and **venire,** which is useful to keep the flow of conversation smooth. The verbs that use **a** **(to)** have been underlined in the list below.

<u>Vado a</u> scuola.	<u>I go to</u> school.
<u>Vado a</u> lavorare.	<u>I go to</u> work.
Tu <u>vai a</u> lavorare oggi?	(Do) <u>you go to</u> work today?
No, <u>vado a</u> fare la spesa.	
	No, <u>I (am) go(ing) to</u> do the grocery shopping.

Esco presto stamattina.　　I go out early this morning.

Esci alle otto oggi?　(Do) you go out at eight today?

Andiamo!	Let's go! (to a group)
Aspetta!	Wait! (fam. command, singular)
Vengo io!	I'm coming!
Vieni qua!	Come here! (fam. command, singular)
Michele, vieni qua!	Michael, come here! (fam. command)

Michele, vieni qua subito!
　　Michael, come here right away!

<u>Io vengo a</u> casa.　　<u>I come</u> home.

Non voglio <u>andare a</u> scuola.
　　I don't want <u>to go to</u> school.

Non voglio <u>venire a</u> casa presto.
　　I don't want <u>to come</u> home early.

Non voglio uscire stasera.
　　I don't want to go out tonight.

Non voglio uscire per cena stasera.
　　I don't want to go out for dinner tonight.

Non voglio uscire con Anna.
　　I don't want to go out with Ann.

Getting Ready

The following expressions are used in the morning when getting up and getting ready for the day. Some phrases are polite expressions we use to greet those living or staying with us, while others describe daily activities. Some of these phrases require Italian reflexive verbs. Italian phrases that use reflexive verbs often do not translate literally into English. Also, the Italian phrases leave out the subject pronouns (**io, tu, lei/lui..**) and put the reflexive pronoun (**mi,ti,si...**) before the conjugated verb! For this page, the Italian subject pronouns are given in parentheses to match the English. For infinitive verbs and familiar command verbs, the Italian pronoun will be attached to the end of the verb, and is given in red.

Getting up in the morning:

(Io) Mi sveglio.   I wake (myself) up.

(Io) Mi alzo.   I get (myself) up.

(Io) Mi alzo presto.   I get (myself) up early.

(Io) Mi alzo <u>alle sei</u>.   I get (myself) up <u>at 6 AM</u>.

(Io) Mi alzo tardi domani.
    I (am going to) get (myself) up late tomorrow.

Chiamami <u>alle nove</u>, per favore.
    Call me <u>at 9 AM</u>, please.

Lasciami stare, per favore!
    Leave me alone (lit. Let me be), please!

Non preoccuparti!   Don't (you) worry (yourself)!

(Io) Mi alzo fra <u>un paio d'ore</u>.
    I (will) get (myself) up in <u>a couple of hours</u>.

(Io) Mi alzo <u>più tardi</u>.
    I (will) get (myself) up <u>a little later</u>.

Conversational Italian for Travelers

<u>Il sabato</u> mi alzo <u>un po' più tardi</u>.
    <u>On Saturdays</u>, I get (myself) up <u>a little bit later</u>.

Buon giorno. <u>Hai dormito</u> bene?
    Good morning. (Did) <u>you sleep</u> well?
             (lit. Have you slept well?)

Si, molto bene, grazie.
    Yes, very well, thank you.

Si, <u>ho dormito</u> molto bene, grazie.
    Yes, <u>I slept</u> very well, thank you.

Vuoi un caffè?	(Do) you want a (cup of) coffee?
Si, vorrei un caffè.	Yes, I would like a coffee.
Si, vorrei del caffè.	Yes, I would like some coffee.
Vuoi del tè?	(Do) you want some tea?
Si, vorrei un tè.	Yes, I would like a (cup of) tea.

No, vorrei un bicchiere di...
    No, I would like a glass of...

                ...acqua.   ...water.

                ...succo d'arancia.   ...orange juice.

Vorrei un biscotto.	I would like a cookie.
Vorrei dei biscotti.	I would like some cookies.

Getting Ready (cont'd)

Getting ready to go out for the day:

Mi faccio il bagno. / Faccio un bagno.
    I take a bath. (lit. I make myself the bath)

Mi faccio la doccia. / Faccio una doccia.
    I take a shower.

Mi faccio una doccia ogni mattina.
    I take a shower every day.

Mi lavo.	I wash myself.
Mi asciugo.	I dry myself off.
Mi pettino.	I comb my hair.
Mi trucco.	I put on my makeup.
Mi faccio la barba.	I shave my beard.
Mi vesto.	I get (myself) dressed.

Mi preparo per il lavoro.
    I get (myself) ready for (the) work.

Mi metto i vestiti.
    I put on my clothes.

Mi metto la giacca e le scarpe.
    I put on my jacket and my shoes.

Mi sento molto bene!   I feel very well!

Vado al lavoro./Vado a lavorare.   I go to work.

At the end of the day:

Torno a casa.   I return home.

Mi tolgo la giacca.   I take off my jacket.

Mi tolgo le scarpe.   I take off my shoes.

Preparo la cena per la famiglia.
     I make the dinner for the family.

Alle nove, mi spoglio.
     At nine, I get (myself) undressed.

Mi metto il pigiama e le ciabatte.
     I put on my pajamas and my slippers.

Mi siedo.   I sit (myself) down.

Mi rilasso.   I relax (myself).

Alle dieci e mezzo, ho sonno.
     At ten thirty, I am sleepy. (lit. I have sleepiness)

Dico a mia figlia, "A nanna! Buona notte!"
     I say to my daughter, "It's night-night! (slang, used
     with children) Good night!"

Mi riposo.   I rest (myself).

Mi addormento.   I fall (myself) asleep.

Dormo bene perché sono stanco(a)!
     I sleep well because I am tired!
         (male/female speaker)

Vocabulary
Hosts and their Guests

There are several Italian words that are commonly used to refer to hosts and their guests that sound very much like their English counterparts. But beware! For instance, in Italian **l'hostess** means **the stewardess** and does not have any other meaning.

L'ospite can be used to refer to **the host** of a party in Italy. However, **l'ospite** is also commonly used to refer to **the guest!**

l'ospite	host / hostess / guest
la padrona di casa	hostess (at her home)
il padrone di casa	host (at his home)
la persona che invita	host or hostess (for event or party outside the home)

l'organizzatore
host / organizer / coordinator
(masculine, for an event or party outside the home)

l'organizzatrice
hostess / organizer / coordinator
(feminine, for an event or party outside the home)

la festa / le feste	holiday(s), celebration(s), party(ies)
la festa di compleanno	birthday party
la festività	religious holiday
fare una festa	to have a party
festeggiare	to celebrate or have a celebration/ to observe a holiday / to party
fare festa	to celebrate / to party

Conversational Italian for Travelers

Meeting and Greeting at a Gathering

In this section are some common expressions that can be used to "break the ice" at a gathering, some simple replies to keep a conversation going, and a few polite phrases of thanks for when it comes time to depart. These are good phrases to commit to memory, as they can be used in many different situations.

Benvenuto! / Benvenuta! / Benvenuti! / Benvenute!
    Welcome! (to a male) / (to a female)/
    (to a group of males, or males + females)/
    (to a group of females only)

Entra!   Come in! (fam. command)

Si accomodi! / Accomodati!
    Make yourself comfortable! (pol./fam. command)

Da questa parte, prego. This way, please.

Si sieda! / Siediti!
    Sit down! (pol./fam. command)

Piacere di conoscerla/conoscerti.
    Pleased to meet you. (pol./fam.)

Piacere mio.   The pleasure is mine.

Lieto(a) di conoscerla/conoscerti.
    Delighted (masc./fem. speaker)
    to meet you. (pol./fam.)

Molto lieto(a)!   Delighted! (masc./fem. speaker)

Sono molto contento(a) di vederla/ti.
    I am very happy (masc./fem. speaker)
    to see you. (pol./fam.)

Meeting and Greeting at a Gathering (cont'd)

Sono felice di rivederla/ti.
 I am happy to see you again. (pol./fam.)

Si ricorda di me? (Do) you remember me? (pol.)

È di questa zona? Are you from around here? (pol.)

Sei di queste parti? Are you from around here? (fam.)

Di che cosa si occupa? What do you do? (pol.)
 (as a job)

Mi occupo di affari. I'm in business.
 (work in a company)

Che lavoro fa/fai? What work do you do? (pol./fam.)

Sono in affari. I am in business.

Sono studente. / Sono studentessa.
 I am a student. (masc./fem. speaker)

Non mi dica!
 You don't say! (lit. You are not telling me!) (pol.)

Sono contento(a) per Lei/te.
 (I) am happy (masc./fem. speaker)
 for you. (pol./fam.)

Mi piace tanto! I love it! / I like it a lot!
 (lit. It is very pleasing to me!)

Mi piace un sacco! I love/like it so much! (idiomatic)
 (lit. It is pleasing to me a sac-full.)

Meraviglioso(a)! Marvelous!/ Wonderful!/ Amazing!

Fantastico(a)! Fantastic!

Devo andare via ora.
    I must leave now.

È stato un piacere.
    It has been a pleasure.

È stato divertente.
    It has been enjoyable/fun/a blast/amusing/funny.

Ti sei divertito(a)?
    (Did) you enjoy yourself? (masc./fem.) (familiar)

Mi sono proprio divertito(a).
    I really enjoyed myself. (masc./fem. speaker)
    (I had a great time.)

Grazie di tutto.
    Thank you for everything.

Grazie per la Sua/la tua ospitalità.
    Thank you for your hospitality. (pol./fam.)

Grazie per una bella serata.
    Thank you for a nice/beautiful/wonderful evening.

La/Ti ringrazio.
    I thank you. (pol./fam.)

Idiomatic Expressions—Polite to Familiar
Dare del tu/Dare del Lei

The verb **dare,** which means **to give,** is used in important idiomatic expressions that allow the change to be made from a formal conversation, using the polite verb form for "you" (the **Lei** form) to a familiar conversation, using the familiar verb form for "you" (the **tu** form).

Imagine, for instance, that a conversation starts up at a gathering between two people who have just met and are about the same age. At some point in the conversation, one will say to the other, **"Diamoci del tu,"** which does not have a good literal translation but roughly means, **"Let's use the familiar form of 'you'** (the **tu** form) **with each other and address each other familiarly."** (The reflexive pronoun **ci** is added to the end of the verb **diamo** in order to refer to **each other.**) This is a familiar way to ask the question, and assumes a level of comfort that the feeling of familiarity will be reciprocated.

An even more familiar way to ask the same question is to use the familiar command form of this phrase, which is, **"Dammi del tu!"** The use of this phrase emphasizes the closeness that the speaker already feels toward the other individual, as familiar command phrases are normally only used between family and close friends or with children.

There are other ways to make this request. If the person making the request wants to continue in the polite way of speaking while the request is being made, and switch only after consent is given, he or she could use the verb **potere** and the very useful phrase of politeness we have come across many times before: **"Mi può..."** In this case, the phrase would be, **"Mi può dare del tu,"** for **"You can use the familiar form of 'you' with me."**

Conversational Italian for Travelers

Or, perhaps one is speaking to an older individual and is not sure the feeling of familiarity will be reciprocated. They can use the same phrase in a question form, as in: "**Le posso dare del tu?**" which means, **"Can I use the familiar form of 'you' with you (pol.)?"**

Finally, it should be noted that Italians use the polite form of "you" in conversation as a way of showing respect to older individuals, teachers, bosses, or those in government. Between Italians, then, situations may arise where someone of importance might feel that another individual is not showing proper respect or has become too familiar with them by their use of the familiar "you" in conversation. In this case, a conversation may start in the familiar but revert to the polite at the request of a superior with the polite command, "**Mi dia del Lei!**" which means, **"Use the polite form of 'you' with me!"**

Below is a summary of these important phrases:

"Diamoci del tu."

"Dammi del tu!"
>   "Let's use the familiar form of 'you' (the tu form) with each other and address each other familiarly."

"Mi può dare del tu."
>   "You can use the familiar form of 'you' with me."

"Le posso dare del tu?"
>   "Can I use the familiar form of 'you' with you?"

"Mi dia del Lei!"
>   "Use the polite form of 'you' with me!"

Shopping

There are many important expressions in Italian that describe the act of shopping. Notice from the tables below how the phrases differ depending on the type of shopping to be done.

Grocery Shopping	
fare la spesa	**to do the grocery shopping** **to do some grocery shopping**

General Shopping	
fare spese	**to do the shopping** (clothes, shoes, or other personal items)
fare compere	**to do the shopping** (any purchase = **la compera**)
fare acquisti	**to do the shopping** (any purchase = **l'acquisto**)
fare shopping	**to do the shopping**

Faccio la spesa. I do the grocery shopping.

Vado a fare la spesa.
    I go to do the grocery shopping.

Faccio compere. I go (lit. do/make) shopping.

Faccio acquisti. I go (lit. do/make) shopping.

Faccio shopping. I go (lit. do/make) shopping.

Faccio shopping di vestiti.
    I go (lit. do/make) shopping for clothes.

Mi può mostrare... Could you show me... (pol.)

| Mi fa vedere... | Could you show me... (pol.) |
| Posso? | May I? |

Che taglia porta?
   What size do you wear? (pol.)

Porto la taglia... / Porto la...
   I take the size... / I take the (size)...

Qual è la taglia italiana per la taglia dieci americana?
   What is the Italian size for (the) size 10 American?

| alla moda | in style |
| di marca | designer / brand name |

Mi provo... / Ti provi...
   I try on (myself)... / You try on (yourself)... (fam.)

Mi metto... / Ti metti...
   I put on (myself)... / You put on (yourself)... (fam.)

Mi metto...	I am trying on (myself)...
	I am going to try on (myself)...
Mi sta bene.	It looks good (lit. stays well) on me.
Ti sta bene.	It looks good (lit. stays well) on you.
Mi va bene.	It fits me well.
La/Lo prendo!	I'll take it! (fem./masc. direct object)

Common Expressions—To Do / To Make
Fare

Many common expressions use the verb **fare,** which means either **to do** or **to make. Fare** can also be used to ask about someone's line of work. The response uses **fare,** followed by the definite article (**il, la, lo, l'**) before the profession.

A note about this, though. In Italy, it can be considered rude to ask someone's occupation right after you have met them. This information usually comes up naturally in conversation and most often is volunteered by the speaker. But, below is a question with **fare** and one of the many answers you may hear:

Che lavoro fai? What work (do) you (fam.) do?

Faccio la dentista. I am a dentist.
(lit. I make work as a dentist.)

Here are some common expressions that use **fare** with the meaning of **to do:**

Ho molto da fare. I am busy/have many (things) to do.

Ho altro da fare. I have other (things) to do.

Non ho niente da fare. I have nothing to do.

Facciamo cosi! Let's do (it) like this!

Non so cosa fare. I don't know what (thing) to do.

Che cosa posso fare per Lei?
What can I do for you? (pol.)

Not all expressions use the literal meaning of **fare**, but some instead stretch the meaning a bit. **Fare** can be used with the meanings of **to cost, to say, to meet,** or, in its reflexive form as **farsi,** when the meaning is **to become/to get.**

Quanto fa?	How much (does) it cost? (the entire purchase)
Fa dieci euro.	It costs 10 euros.
Facciamo alle otto.	Let's make it/do (it) at 8 o'clock.
Si fa tardi.	It's getting late.
Si fa buio.	It's getting dark.

There are many other expressions which involve performing an activity that use **fare.** These expressions are translated into English with the verb **to take.**

Vado a fare un giro in macchina.
    I go to take a drive in the car.

Faccio un giro in macchina.   I take a drive.

Faccio due passi.
    I take a short stroll. (lit. I take two steps.)

Faccio un salto da Maria.
    I drop by (lit. take a hop over to) Maria's.

Faccio un viaggio.   I take a trip.

Faccio una foto/fotografia.   I take a picture.

Posso fare una foto?   May I take a picture?

Mi può fare una foto?
    Could you take a picture of/for me?

Making Friends

Now you are in Italy and have decided to stay for awhile. You may meet someone you want to get to know better. What should you say to break the ice?

Or, maybe you are just trying to enjoy a coffee, and someone introduces themselves. What to say if you are interested?

Here are some common English phrases that can be used to compliment a person you may want to approach, translated into familiar Italian (some just for fun and others more serious). To follow are some replies—if you are interested—or not!

Let's get to know one another:

CITY LIFE

Mi scusi...   Excuse me... (pol.)

Scusa...   Excuse me... (fam.)

Credo che ci siamo già visiti prima...
da qualche parte?
> Haven't we seen (already met) each other before...
> around here?

Penso di conoscerti già.
> I think that I've met you before.

Hai degli occhi molto belli!
> You have beautiful eyes!

Tu hai il viso della Madonna.
> You have a beautiful face.
> (lit. the face of Mother Mary)

Che cosa fai... per il resto della tua vita?
> What are you doing... for the rest of your life?

Or, a little less flowery:

È libero questo posto?   Is this seat free?

Ti dispiace se mi siedo qui?

         Would you mind if I sit here?

Posso sedermi con te?   May I sit with you?

Ti piace questo posto?   Do you like this place?

Ti stai divertendo?   Are you enjoying yourself?

Con chi sei?   Who are you with?

Sono da sola(o).
    I am alone. (fem./masc. speaker)

Sono con un'amica/un amico.
    I am with a friend. (female friend/male friend)

Sto aspettando qualcuno.
    I am waiting for someone.

Sei sposata(o)?   Are you married? (to female/male)

Sei single?*   Are you single?*

Sei divorziata(o)?   Are you divorced? (to female/male)

Cosa prendi?   What are you having?

Posso offrirti qualcosa da bere?
    May I offer to you something to drink?

Vuoi qualcosa da bere / da mangiare?
    (Do) you want something to drink / to eat?

*Although the English word **single** is commonly used in Italian conversation, the Italian words for single are **nubile** for a **woman** and **celibe** for a **man.**

Making Friends (cont'd)

Let's get together... The following expressions are useful to arrange a meeting with a new friend. (Also see the underlined phrases. This is a good way to learn those Italian prepositions!)

Perché non ci vediamo? Let's get together.
(lit. Why don't we get together/see each other?)

Posso avere il tuo...	May I have your...
...numero di telefono?	...telephone number?
...indirizzo email?	...email address?

Hai tempo domani?
　　Do you have time tomorrow?

Posso rivederti domani?
　　May I see you again tomorrow?

Sei libera(o)...	Are you free (to female/male)...
...domani?	...tomorrow?
...domani sera?	...tomorrow night?
...la settimana prossima?	...next week?

Vuoi andare...	Do you want to go...
...<u>al</u> <u>ristorante</u>?	...to a restaurant?
...<u>al</u> <u>bar</u>?	...to a (coffee) bar?
...<u>al</u> <u>café</u>?	...to a cafe?
...<u>in pizzeria</u>?	...to a pizzeria?

Posso invitarla/ti a cena?
>May I invite you to dinner? (pol./fam.)

Ti piacerebbe... / Vuoi...
>Would you like to... / (Do) you want to...

...andare in piazza?   ...go to the piazza?

...andare in chiesa?   ...go to church?

...andare al cinema?   ...go to the movies?

...andare al concerto?   ...go to the concert?

...andare allo spettacolo?   ...go to the show?
                                  (performance)

...andare alla mostra?   ...go to the show? (exhibit)

...andare al museo?   ...go to the museum?

...andare a ballare?   ...go dancing?

Ti piacerebbe... / Vuoi...
>Would you like to... / (Do) you want to...

venire con noi...   come with us...

...in spiaggia / al mare?   ...to the beach / to the sea?

...in montagna?   ...to the mountains?

...in campagna?   ...to the countryside?

Making Friends (cont'd)

And the answer is... no. (politely)

Mi dispiace, ma...	I am sorry, but...
...domani non posso.	...I can't tomorrow.
...domani non va bene.	...tomorrow is not good.

Ho molto (lavoro) da fare.
   I have a lot (of work) to do.

Sono occupata(o) domani sera.
   I am busy (fem./masc. speaker) tomorrow night.

Ho un altro impegno.
   I have another commitment.

Ho un altro appuntamento.
   I have another appointment / date.

Ho un ragazzo / una ragazza.
   I have a boyfriend / girlfriend.

Ho un fidanzato / una fidanzata.
   I have a fiancé / fiancée.
   (steady boyfriend / steady girlfriend)
   (engaged to be married to male/female)

Conversational Italian for Travelers

If you need to leave someone's company because you are not feeling well, or just have to leave quickly...

Non mi sento bene.
    I don't feel well.

Sono molto stanca(o).
    I am very tired. (fem./masc. speaker)

Ho un (gran) mal di testa.
    I have a (severe/bad) headache.

Non sono sicura(o) se posso...
    I am not sure if I can... (fem./masc. speaker)

Chiamami più tardi/domani.
    Call me a little later/tomorrow.

Devo (proprio) andare adesso.
    I (really) have to go now.

Vorrei tornare a casa.
    I want to go back home.

And the answer is... no! (not so politely)

Ho di meglio da fare.	I have better things to do.
Lasciami in pace!	Leave me in peace!
Lasciami stare!	Leave me alone! (lit. Leave me be!)
Vai, cammina!	Go, (take) a walk!
Vai via!	Go away!

Making Friends (cont'd)

And the answer is... yes!

Sì, sono libera(o).	Yes, I am free. (fem./masc. speaker)
Lei è molto gentile.	You are very nice. (pol.)
Che bella idea!	What a wonderful idea!
Com'è bello!	How nice!
Mi piacerebbe molto.	I would like (it) very much.
Volentieri!	I'd love to! (lit. certainly, gladly)

Dove ci incontriamo?
  Where should we meet (each other)?

Posso passare a prenderla/ti?
  Can I pick you up? (pol./fam.)

A che ora posso venire a prenderla/ti?
  At what time can I come to get you? (pol./fam.)

La vengo a prendere alle otto (in punto).
  I (will) come to pick you up at 8 (o'clock). (pol.)

Vengo a prenderti alle otto.
  I (will) come to pick you up at 8 (o'clock). (fam.)

La/Ti chiamerò alle otto.
  I will call you at 8 (o'clock). (pol./fam.)

Non vedo l'ora di vederti!
  I can't wait to see you! (fam. idiomatic expression)

La ringrazio molto.
  I thank you very much. (pol.)

Ti ringrazio molto.
  I thank you very much. (fam.)

Conversational Italian for Travelers

Grammar Note
Friendship and More

l'amicizia	friendship
fare amicizia	to make friends
tutti(e) e due	both of you / the two of them
entrambi i ragazzi	both of the boys
entrambe le ragazze	both of the girls
l'amico	the friend (male)
gli amici	the friends (male group) or (male + female group)
l'amica	the friend (girl)
le amiche	the girlfriends (female group)
il mio migliore amico	my best friend (only one)
il mio amico del cuore	my close friend

l'amore	love
Sono innamorato(a).	I am in love. (masc./fem.)
Mi vuoi bene?	Do you love me/care for me?
Mi ami?	Do you love me? (romantic)
Si, ti voglio bene.	Yes, I love you. / I care for you.
Si, ti amo.	Yes, I love you. (romantic)
Ti amerò per sempre.	I will love you forever.

Voglio stare con te per sempre.
> I want to stay with you forever.

Common Expressions—Well, Fine, Good
Bene vs. Buono

Bene is an important Italian adverb that denotes how one is feeling and has the meaning of **well** or **fine**. **Buono,** with its variations **buona(i,e)**, is an adjective that means **good.** See the "Meeting and Greeting" phrases (page 9) and below for important expressions that use **bene** and **buono.**

In English, we often use the word "good" in place of an adverb. For instance, how many times have you asked someone, "How are you feeling?" and received the answer, "Good"? It is likely that anyone living in America today has heard "good" in response to this question many more times than the English adverb "well" or "fine." In Italian, this is not the case, however, as **bene** is consistently used.

Bene can also be used as the equivalent of **OK,** with the common expression, "**Va bene.**" After only a few days in Italy, it is likely you will hear the question, "**Come va?**" for "**How's it going?**" and its usual answer, "**Va bene,**" for "**It's going well./It's fine./OK.**"

Va bene.	It's going well. / It's fine. / OK.
piuttosto bene	pretty well / pretty good
abbastanza bene	well enough
proprio bene	really well / very well
tutto bene	all right
tutto va bene	all is well
nota bene	note well / please note
Buon viaggio!	Have a good trip!

Conversational Italian for Travelers

Common Expressions—Love
Bene

An additional use for the adverb **bene** is found with the phrase, **"Ti voglio bene,"** which translates as, **"I wish you well,"** or **"I care for you."** In the past, Italians would also use this phrase to mean **"I love you"** in a romantic way, instead of the verb that means **to love,** which is **amare** (as anyone who watches older Italian movies can attest).

Today, the phrase, **"Ti voglio bene,"** is most often used for platonic love among family members and close friends, while the verb **amare** is usually* reserved for romantic love. So, if someone special asks you, **"Mi vuoi bene?" "Do you care for me/love me?"** or **"Mi ami?" "Are you in love with me?"** here are some replies:

Ti voglio bene.	I like you. / I care for you. (platonic)
Ti voglio bene.	I love you. (romantic)
Ti amo.	I love you. (romantic)
amare	to love
amore / amore mio	love / my love
tesoro mio	my treasure
stella mia	my star

Finally, some phrases if you have fallen out of love:

Non ti voglio più bene.
    I don't like/care for you anymore.

Non ti amo più.
    I don't love you anymore.

*Use of **amare** has become more universal in Italy, similar to "love" in America, and is now sometimes used to refer to things.

Vocabulary
Making a Telephone Call

il telefono	telephone
il telefono pubblico*	public telephone*
il telefonino / il cellulare	cell phone
la segreteria telefonica	voice mail or answering machine
il messaggio in segreteria	message left on voice mail or an answering machine
dare un colpo di telefono	to give a hit/call with the telephone (slang)
squillare	to ring out loud (as in a telephone or door bell)
uno squillo	ringing tone indicating telephones are connected
Rispondi al telefono!	Answer/Pick up the phone! (fam. command)
Metti giù il telefono!	Hang up the phone! (fam. command)
la linea	telephone line
il segnale di libero	dial tone
il segnale di occupato	busy signal
La linea è libera.	The (telephone) line is free.
La linea è occupata.	The (telephone) line is busy.
Resti in linea!	Hold the line! (pol. command)
È caduta la linea.	The line dropped/disconnected.

il numero di telefono	telephone number
il numero sbagliato	wrong number
il numero di fax	fax number
il prefisso telefonico	area code (for US phone numbers) / country code
fare il prefisso	dial the area code/ country code
fare una telefonata	to make a telephone call
telefonare	to make a telephone call
fare uno squillo	to make a telephone call
fare il numero	to dial the number
il numero verde	the toll free number (lit. the green line)
il/la centralista	operator (male/female)

Vorrei fare un appagamento.
   I would like to make a collect call.

Vorrei fare a carico del destinatario.
   I would like to make a collect call.

Vorrei fare una telefonata interurbana.
   I would like to make a long distance call.

*A few public telephones still exist in Italy today!

Making a Telephone Call (cont'd)

When making a telephone call to a friend at their house, the initial greeting might go something like this:

Pronto. Sono Caterina.	Ready. (for hello) I am Kathy.
Pronto. Sono io!	Ready. (for hello) It's me! (lit. It is I!)
Posso parlare con Pietro?	May I speak with Peter?
Pietro è a casa?	Is Peter at home?
C'è Pietro?	Is Peter there?

When calling a business associate at their office, you might begin by saying:

Pronto. Sono il signor / la signora / la signorina Rossi.
   Hello. I am Mr. / Mrs. / Miss. Rossi.

Vorrei parlare con il signor Manzini.
   I would like to speak with Mr. Manzini.

Mi può passare il direttore, per piacere?*
   Can you put me through to (give me) the director, please? (pol.)*

Me lo può passare?* / Me la può passare?*

   Can you put him/her through to me? (pol.)*

**If you are speaking to a colleague, you can use the familiar phrases: "Mi puoi passare..." or "Me lo/la puoi passare?"

A receptionist at a business might answer the phone with the following questions:

Pronto. Che cosa posso fare per Lei?
    Hello. What can I do for you? (pol.)

Posso aiutarla?   May I help you? (pol.)

Chi parla?   Who is speaking? (pol.)

Chi chiama?   Who is calling? (pol.)

When requesting to speak to a business associate, you may hear the following replies:

Resti in linea, per favore.
    Hold (the line), please. (pol. command)

Mi dispiace, ma...   I'm sorry, but...

...il direttore è occupato.
    ...the director is busy.

...il direttore non c'è oggi.
    ...the director is not in today.

...il direttore è (appena) uscito(a).
    ...the director has (just) stepped out. (masc./fem.)

...il direttore è in riunione.
    ...the director is (attending) in a meeting.

Glielo passo. / Gliela passo.
    I'll put him/her through to you. (pol.)

Making a Telephone Call (cont'd)

Less formal replies for calls made to a home:

Sì, aspetta un momento.	Yes, wait a moment.
Sì, aspetta un attimo.	Yes, wait a second.
Te lo/la passo.	I'll put him/her through to you.
No, non è in casa.	No, (he/she) is not at home.
No, non c'è.	No, (he /she) is not here.

If you want to try to get some information or leave a message, you might ask:

Quando torna lui/lei?   When (will) he/she return?

Sa quando torna lui/lei?
  (Do) you know when he/she (will) return? (pol.)

Può dirgli/dirle di chiamarmi?
  Can you tell (to) him/her to call me? (pol.)

Può dirgli/dirle che ho chiamato?
  Can you tell (to) him/her that I called? (pol.)

Può prendere un messaggio?
  Can you take a message? (pol.)

Posso richiamare più tardi?
  Can I call back later?

Richiamerei (un po') più tardi.
  I would like to call back (a little) later.

Richiamerò (un po') più tardi.
  I will call back (a little) later.

Ending a telephone conversation with someone you know:

Ci sentiamo...
    We will speak to each other... (lit. hear each other)

...più tardi /dopo / presto. ...later / later / soon.

Devo scappare!	I must run! (lit. escape/run away)
Richiamami!	Call me back! (fam. command)
Chiamami!	Call me! (fam. command)
Fatti sentire!	Let me hear from you! (lit. Make yourself heard!)

If you don't understand the reply or are having trouble hearing the Italian, you might say:

Non capisco bene.	I don't understand well.
Può/Puoi ripetere?	Can you repeat? (pol./fam.)
Che vuole/vuoi dire?	What do you mean to say? (pol./fam.)
Come si dice?	How does one say (it)?
Che ha/hai detto?	What did you say? (pol./fam.)
Che significa?	What (does that) mean?
Non ti sento molto bene.	I don't hear you very well.
Parla a voce più alta.	Speak a little louder.

Leaving/Sending a Message

Phrases you may hear on voice mail or an answering machine:

La casella vocale/segreteria telefonica di...
> The voice mailbox/answering machine of...

Non posso/possiamo rispondere al telefono ora.
> I/We cannot answer the phone now.

Lasciate il vostro messaggio, e il vostro nome, la data, e l'ora della vostra chiamata...
> Leave your message, and your name, the date, and the time of your call...

...e il vostro numero di telefono
> ...and your telephone number

...dopo il segnale acustico.
> ...after the beep.

Vi richiamerò/Vi richiameremo presto.
> I/We will call you all back soon.

How to leave a message:

Sono la signora Manzini.	I am Mrs. Manzini.
Sono Caterina.	I am Kathy.
Vorrei parlare di...	I want to talk about...
Possiamo parlare di...	Can we talk about...

Oggi è lunedì tre agosto, alle dieci.
> Today is Monday, August third, at 10 AM.

Il mio numero di telefono è...
> My telephone number is...

For today's world, where cell phones make instant messaging and emailing an easy and a common occurrence, below are some additional phrases in Italian:

la segretaria telefonica	voice mail
il messaggio (di testo)	text message
la posta elettronica / la mail	email
l'indirizzo email/mail	email address
chiocciola	@sign (lit. snail)

orders chiocciola Stella Lucente punto com =
    orders@stellalucente.com

mandare / spedire un messaggio
    to send a text message / to text someone

mandare via mail
    to send by email

inviare un'email / una mail
    to send an email

controllare un messaggio / un'email / una mail
    to check a text message /an email

Controlla la tua mail!   Check your email! (fam. com.)

La mia amica mi ha mandato un messaggio.
    My friend sent a text message to me.

È arrivato un messaggio.
    You have a message. (lit. A message has arrived.)

Ho ricevuto un messaggio.
    I have (received) a message.

Hotel Reservations

la camera / la stanza	room
la camera singola	room with a single bed
la camera matrimoniale	room with a double bed
le camere adiacenti	adjacent rooms
il letto	bed
il letto supplementare	additional bed
disponibile	available
al completo	completely booked / full
la prenotazione	reservation

Vorrei... / Desidero...	I would like... / I want to...

...fare una prenotazione.
   ...make a reservation.

...annullare una prenotazione.
   ...cancel a reservation.

...cambiare una prenotazione.
   ...change a reservation.

...controllare una prenotazione.
   ...check a reservation.

...confermare una prenotazione.
   ...confirm a reservation.

...ordinare la prima colazione.
   ...order breakfast.

Conversational Italian for Travelers

Grammar Note
Making, Checking, and Changing a Reservation

The noun that refers to a hotel reservation is **la prenotazione**. The Italian verbs **prenotare** and **riservare** translate into English as **"to make/book a reservation."** The use of these Italian verbs and noun varies with the situation.

Most commonly, when asking to make a reservation at a hotel, on a train, or at the theater, Italians use the noun **prenotazione** with the verb **fare** and **"make a reservation,"** which is **"fare una prenotazione."**

When boarding a train or entering a theater with a ticket that has a reserved seat, one would have **"un biglietto con la prenotazione"** or **"a ticket with the reservation."** To say you are checking your seat, use the phrase, **"Controllo il biglietto con la prenotazione"** for **"I am checking the ticket with the reservation."**

However, the actual seat on a train, theater, or room in a hotel is referred to as "reserved" as in, **"Il posto è riservato."** The seat or room has been booked, and no one else can use it. If someone else has made a **prenotazione** before you, your request might be denied due to **una camera riservata, una stanza riservata,** or **un posto riservato.**

To cancel a reservation, use the verb **annullare** and say, **"Vorrei annullare una prenotazione,"** for **"I would like to cancel a reservation."** Or, if a reservation needs to be changed, use the verb **cambiare,** as in, **"Vorrei cambiare una prenotazione."**

Vocabulary
At the Hotel

il viaggiatore	traveler (masc.)
la viaggiatrice	traveler (fem.)
l'albergo	hotel
l'albergatore	hotel manager (masc.)
l'albergatrice	hotel manager (fem.)
la pensione	boarding house/bed and breakfast
l'ostello (della gioventù)	youth hostel
il pernottamento	overnight stay
la pensione completa	
room and board (includes three meals a day)	
la mezza pensione	
room, breakfast, and one meal (half board)	
il/la receptionist	receptionist (masc./fem.)
la reception	front desk (reception)
il facchino	porter
il portiere / il portinaio	doorman / porter
il concierge	concierge
la portineria	concierge / caretaker
il servizio di portineria	concierge services
il parcheggiatore	parking attendant
la cameriera	maid
servizio in camera	room service

Conversational Italian for Travelers

il portone	main entrance
l'atrio	lobby
l'ingresso	entrance
l'entrata	entrance
l'uscita	exit
l'uscita di emergenza	emergency exit
l'uscita di sicurezza	fire exit
divieto di uscita	no exit (forbidden to exit)
l'ascensore	elevator
le scale	stairs
il corridoio	hallway
il salone	hotel dining room
la piscina	swimming pool
la sauna	sauna
la vasca idromassaggio	jacuzzi
il campo da golf	golf course
il campo da tennis	tennis court

Vocabulary
In the Hotel Room

il letto	bed
il comodino	night table
la televisione / la TV	television / TV
la TV via cavo	cable TV
la TV via satellite	satellite TV
l'orologio	clock
la radiosveglia	alarm clock
il canale	TV channel
il telecomando	remote control
la pila / la batteria	battery
la chiave	key
la chiave magnetica	key card
la serratura	lock
chiuso a chiave	locked (with a key)
controllare	to check / take care of
rifare la camera	to make-up a room
rompere	to break
riparare	to repair
la connessione	the connection
l'accesso a Internet	Internet access

il collegamento ad Internet
   connection to the Internet

Conversational Italian for Travelers

il lavandino	bathroom sink
il rubinetto	faucet
l'acqua calda/fredda	hot/cold water
l'asciugamano	towel
il telo da spiaggia	beach towel
il gabinetto	toilet bowl
la carta igienica	toilet paper
il sapone	soap
l'aria condizionata	air conditioning
il riscaldamento	heating
la cassaforte	safe
l'elettricità	electricity
l'asciugacapelli	hair dryer
il rasoio elettrico	electric razor
lo shampoo	shampoo
la lozione	lotion
la lozione dopobarba	after shave
la spazzola	brush
il pettine	comb
lo spazzolino dei denti	toothbrush
il dentifricio	toothpaste

Vocabulary
The Weather

le previsioni del tempo	weather forecast
la temperatura	temperature
il grado	degree
il sole	sun
sereno(a)	clear, without clouds
mite	mild
nuvoloso(a)	cloudy
la nuvola	cloud
bagnato(a)	wet
la pioggia	rain
la tempesta	storm
il tuono e il lampo	thunder and lightening
l'arcobaleno	rainbow
il vento	wind
la brezza	cool breeze
l'aria	air
il caldo	heat
l'umidità	humidity
afoso(a)	muggy / humid
la stella	star
la luna	moon

Conversational Italian for Travelers

Vocabulary
Sightseeing

il/la turista	tourist (masc./fem.)
i turisti / le turiste	tourists (masc./fem. groups)
l'agenzia turistica	travel agency
la guida turistica	tourist guide
la galleria	(art) gallery covered shopping mall
l'opera	job / creative work musical theater
la mostra	show / exhibit
il duomo	cathedral
la chiesa	church
la città vecchia	the old city / old town
il ponte vecchio	the old bridge (Florence)
il giro	tour / excursion
il giro turistico	sightseeing tour
la gita	outing / excursion
l'avventura	adventure /ordeal /escapade
la visita	visit / tour
l'itinerario	itinerary / schedule
il programma	plan / program
l'orario	schedule
la macchina fotografica	camera
la fotografia / la foto	photograph / photo

Just the Important Phrases

Finding One's Way and Directions

Most Italians are quite friendly and helpful to tourists, especially if a polite phrase is used to initiate the conversation, such as, **"Mi scusi"** or **"Per favore."** Once you have someone's attention, the verb **può...?** (**"could you...?"** from **potere**), followed by an infinitive verb, will enable you to ask politely for whatever you need.

Some examples we have already encountered include the phrases, **"Mi può dire?"** (**"Could you tell me?"**) and **"Mi può portare?"** (**"Could you take me?"**). Remember that **"Può chiamare...?"** means, **"Could you call...?"** a taxi, for instance, or a person. We revisit this polite verb **può** in the list below as we ask for directions!

The polite verb **"Sa...?"** (**"Do you know?"** from **sapere**) is also useful to ask someone if they know the information we need. And, of course, a nice way to end the conversation would be to say, **"Mille grazie!"**

Mi scusi, mi può dire...
>   Excuse me, could you (pol.) tell me...

...dov'è il duomo?   ...where is the cathedral?

...dov'è la galleria?   ...where is the shopping mall?

Sa dov'è il museo?
>   (Do) you (pol.) know where the museum is?

Cerco... / Cerchiamo...
>   I am looking for... / We are looking for...

Ho/Abbiamo bisogno di indicazioni.
>   I/We need directions.

Conversational Italian for Travelers

Ho/Abbiamo bisogno di un'informazione.*
   I/We need information.

Sa come arrivare a...?
   (Do) you (pol.) know how to get to...?

Vado bene per...?
   Am I going the right way for...?

No, sta andando nella direzione sbagliata.
   No, you are going in the wrong direction.

È lontano da qui?	Is it far from here?
È vicino da qui?	Is it close to here?
A quanta dista?	How far is (it)?
Quant'è lontano da...?	How far is (it) from...?

A quanti chilometri è da...?
   How many kilometers is it from...?

Quanto tempo a piedi?   How long (walking) on foot?

Deve camminare per un'isolato.
   You must walk for one block.

Mi sono perso(a).	I am lost. (masc./fem.)
Come si arriva a...?	How do I (does one) get to...?
È questa la strada per...?	*Is this the road/street for...?
Deve seguire per...	You must follow for...
Deve proseguire per...	. You must continue for...

Finding One's Way and Directions (cont'd)

Come si chiama questa strada?
  What is the name of this road/street?

Dove porta questa strada?
  Where (does) this road/street go? (lit. take me)

Grazie mille (per l'informazione*).
  Thank you very much (for the information).

l'indicazione / le indicazioni	direction / directions
la strada / la via / la calle	street / road
sull'altro lato della strada	across the street
quella via	that way / that street
l'isolato	city block
all'angolo	at the corner
dietro l'angolo	around the corner
l'incrocio	intersection
verso	toward
lontano da	away from
fino alla fine	to the end
sempre diritto	straight ahead

*One piece of information is **un'informazione** or **l'informazione**; for more than one piece of information use the plural: **le informazioni.**

Grammar Note
Adverbial Prepositions and Directions

vicino a	near / beside / next to
lontano da	far from
là / lì	there
di là	over there
laggiù / lassù	down there / up there
davanti a	in front of / before
di fronte a	in front of
(di) dietro	behind / after
dentro	in / inside
fuori di	outside / out of
sopra	on top of / above
su	on / upon
sotto	under / below / underneath
girare	to turn / to tour / to travel through
giri a destra	you turn right (pol. command)
giri a sinistra	you turn left (pol. command)
scenda	you go down (pol. command)
attraversi	you go across (pol. command)
attraversare la strada	to cross the street

Speaking with the Waiter

Here are some expressions that are commonly used when dining in a restaurant. The **io** (**I**) and **noi** (**we**) forms of the verbs **potere** (**to can**) and **volere** (**to want**) are important to know in this situation, since requests are usually made for oneself or for the entire table.

We revisit the verb "**Può?**" for a polite way to say, "**Could you?**" and add "**Posso?**" for "**May I?**" and "**Possiamo?**" for "**May we?**" to our list of polite phrases to use when making a request.

To the popular phrase, "**Io vorrei...**" for "**I would like...**" we add the conditional plural form, "**Noi vorremmo...**" for "**We would like...**"

Upon entering a restaurant, begin with:
Buona sera.   Good evening.

Abbiamo una prenotazione per due persone per le otto.
We have a reservation for two people for 8 o'clock.

Posso... / Possiamo...   May I... / May we...

   ...sedermi/sederci vicino alla finestra?
     ...sit by the window?

   ...sedermi/sederci a un altro tavolo?
     ...sit at another table?

   ...avere il menù?
     ...see (have) the menu?

Qual è lo speciale oggi/stasera?
   What is the special today/this evening?

Che cosa ha scelto/avete scelto?
   What have you/you all chosen? (pol.)

Conversational Italian for Travelers

Vorrei... / Vorremmo...   I would like... / We would like...

...per antipasto, l'insalata mista.
   ...for the antipasto course, mixed salad.

...per primo, le tagliatelle alla bolognese.
   ...for the first course, tagliatelle with meat sauce.

...per secondo, l'ossobuco.
   ...for the second course, braised veal shank.

...per dolce, solamente frutta.
   ...for dessert, only fruit.

Non posso mangiare niente...
   I cannot eat anything...

...fatto con noci/arachidi.
   ...made with nuts/peanuts.

...molto piccante.
   ...very spicy.

Mi può portare...   Could you bring me... (pol.)

Ci può portare...   Could you bring us... (pol.)

...dell'acqua naturale?
   ...some still water/natural water?

...dell'acqua frizzante?
   ...some sparkling water?

...del pane / più pane?
   ...some bread / more bread?

...il conto, per favore.   ...the check, please.

Breakfast, Lunch and Dinner

Here are some common expressions that may come up in general conversation when talking about meals. Much of Italian life revolves around meeting others to enjoy food together, as this is considered part of **"la dolce vita"** (**the good life**), so these phrases should come in handy while you are enjoying your time in Italy!

Andiamo a cena fuori domani sera?
    Are we going out to dinner tomorrow night?

Andiamo sempre a cena fuori?
    Are we still going out to dinner?

Andiamo ancora a cena fuori?
    Are we going out to dinner again?

Mi piacerebbe offrirti una cena.
    I would like to treat you to dinner.

Una cena offerta da...   A dinner offered by the...

cena per due   dinner for two

È l'ora di cena.   (It) is dinnertime.

La cena è pronta.   Dinner is ready.

il dopocena   after dinner

Cosa c'è per pranzo?
    What's for lunch?

Ho portato il mio pranzo.
    I brought my lunch.

pranzo al sacco   bag lunch

pranzo di lavoro   business lunch

If you would like to write or email an invitation to friends or business associates for dinner, the following may be helpful.

Vorrei invitarti...   I would like to invite you (fam.)...

Vorrei invitarvi...   I would like to invite you all...

Sono lieto(a) di invitarla a cena...
> I am delighted (male/female speaker)
> to invite you to dinner... (pol.)

Sono lieto(a) di invitarVi* a cena...
> I am delighted (male/female speaker)
> to invite you all to dinner... (pol. to a group)

...al ristorante.   ...at the restaurant.

...a casa mia.   ...at my house.

...che si terrà (il giorno) alle (ore).
> ...which will be held on (the day) at the (hour).

R.S.V.P.**   Please respond.
             The courtesy of a reply is requested.

***Voi** with a capital letter **V** can be used in modern Italian when addressing a group of acquaintances as **"you all"** when one wants to be a bit formal or classy. This form has come into use more frequently now that the ultra-formal **Loro** is rarely used as the polite "you all" form.

** From the French phrase: **Répondez s'il vous plaît.**

Just the Important Phrases   87

Vocabulary
Ordering at the Restaurant
Table Setting and Drinks

il ristorante	restaurant
la trattoria	family-style restaurant
l'osteria / l'enoteca	tavern / wine shop
il primo	first course
il secondo	second course
il dolce	dessert
il ristoratore	restaurateur (owner)
il cuoco / la cuoca	cook (masc./fem.)
il capocuoco / lo chef	chef
il cameriere / l a cameriera	waiter / waitress
il menù	menu
il piatto del giorno	specialty of the day
la specialità dello chef	the chef's specialty
la specialità della casa	the specialty of the house
il tavolo / la tavola	table / table set for a meal
la tovaglia	tablecloth
il piatto	plate
il tovagliolo	(cloth) napkin
la forchetta	fork
il cucchiaio	teaspoon

il coltello	knife
il bicchiere	glass
il bicchiere da vino	wine glass
la tazza	cup
il piattino	saucer
l'acqua minerale	mineral water
l'acqua gassata	carbonated water
l'acqua naturale	non-carbonated water
le bibite	soft drinks
la limonata	lemonade
l'aranciata	orange soda
l'orzata	almond drink
l'amarena	cherry drink
(un) tè freddo	iced tea*
(un) caffè freddo	iced coffee*
(un) tè caldo	hot tea
il latte	milk
la panna	cream for coffee
lo zucchero	sugar
il sale e pepe	salt and pepper

*Most restaurants and hotels in Italy do not have ice making machines and therefore do not put ice into their "iced drinks."

Vocabulary
Appetizers

l'antipasto – the appetizer course

gli antipasti – the appetizers

il pane – bread

una fetta di pane – a slice of bread

la bruschetta – toasted bread slices rubbed with garlic (pronounced: **broo/SKE/ta**) topped with chopped tomatoes or chopped liver, etc.

l'olio (d'oliva) – olive oil

l'aceto – vinegar – Balsamic vinegar (aged vinegar from Modena) or red wine vinegar

l'antipasto misto – assorted appetizers

l'insalata verde/mista – lettuce and fresh vegetables

i calamari fritti – fried squid

la panzanella – tomato and bread salad; usually made with left-over or stale bread

l'insalata Caprese – fresh tomato and buffalo mozzarella slices, layered with fresh basil, and drizzled with olive oil, from the island of Capri

le olive – olives

le verdure (sottaceto) – vegetables (pickled)

i peperoni (sottaceto) – peppers (pickled)

i funghi (sottaceto) – mushrooms (pickled)

i carciofi (sottolio) – artichoke hearts (in olive oil)

la caponata – Sicilian cooked eggplant and olive appetizer, served cold

le acciughe – anchovies

la bagna càuda – warm olive oil, garlic and anchovy dip for fresh or boiled vegetables, from Piedmont region of Northern Italy

le sardine – sardines

la mortadella – special type of baloney, from the city of Bologna

il salame/i salumi – salami – dried or smoke-cured meats; varies vary by region

il fritto misto – assorted batter-fried vegetables, assorted fried fish and seafood, or a combination of both fried vegetables and fried seafood

il prosciutto (di Parma) – special air-dried/cured ham, from the city of Parma

prosciutto e melone – special cured ham served on top of a cantaloupe slice, often drizzled with balsamic vinegar

lo speck – special smoked ham, from the region of Tyrol in Austria

il formaggio – cheese – made from cow, sheep, or goat's milk; varies by region

Vocabulary
Pasta and Gnocchi

Pasta fresca, fatta in casa — Fresh pasta, homemade (flour and water with eggs)

Made from pasta dough rolled out into thin sheets and then cut into different shapes by hand.

le tagliatelle / le fettuccine – long, flat pasta

le pappardelle – wide, long, flat pasta

le lasagne – rectangular shaped, wide pasta for a casserole

le penne – short, rolled tubular pasta with angled ends (lit. pens/quill pens)

pasta alla chitarra – ancient method from Abruzzo region to make spaghetti by rolling dough over a wooden box strung with wires

i ravioli – pasta squares stuffed with cheese, vegetables (usually spinach or squash), or meat

i tortellini – pasta squares, stuffed with cheese or meat, and then folded and shaped to look like the navel of the goddess Venus

i cappelletti – pasta rounds, stuffed with cheese or meat, and then folded and shaped to look like small hats

Pasta secca — Dried pasta (flour and water)

Made from pasta dough extruded through a pasta machine with special molds that create different shapes.

gli spaghetti / uno spaghetto – long strands of round pasta / one strand of pasta

i vermicelli – long, thin strands of round pasta (lit. little worms)

i bucatini – very thick strands of round pasta with a central hole

le linguine – long, flat pasta

i fusilli – spiral-shaped strands of pasta

i maccheroni – macaroni; general term for short pasta of various shapes made by machine molds, which can resemble common items, like shells, elbows, or stars

i rigatoni – tubular pasta with ridges

gli ziti – tubular pasta without ridges

le conchiglie – shell-shaped pasta

gli gnocchi / uno gnocco* – small, ridged dumplings, most often made from cooked potatoes combined with flour and water (and sometimes with egg)

*Gnocco can mean **dummy.** Only in northern Italy, **gnocco** can also mean **handsome.**

Just the Important Phrases

Vocabulary
Famous Italian Pasta, Gnocchi and Rice Dishes

Tagliatelle/Pappardelle con Bolognese Ragù
Fresh ribbon pasta with a meat ragout, from Bologna

Ragù alla Bolognese
Beef, veal, and sausage meats cooked slowly with finely chopped onion, celery, carrot, and wine, enriched with butter and cream, from Bologna

Lasagne alla Bolognese
Lasagna pasta layered with béchamel sauce and Bolognese sauce and then baked in a casserole, from Bologna

Spaghetti all'Aglio, Olio, e Peperoncino
Spaghetti with garlic, extra-virgin olive oil, and chili peppers, from Campania

Spaghetti alla Carbonara
Spaghetti with egg, Italian bacon (guanciale), Peccorino Romano cheese and pepper, from Rome

Spaghetti Cacio e Pepe
Spaghetti with only Peccorino Romano cheese and pepper, from Rome

Spaghetti al Nero (di Seppia)
Spaghetti with cuttlefish (squid) black ink sauce, popular in Venice and Sicily

Spaghetti al Pomodoro
Spaghetti with fresh or lightly cooked tomatoes

Spaghetti alla Puttanesca
Spaghetti with tomatoes, anchovies and olives, as a prostitute would make

Spaghetti al Sugo
Spaghetti with sauce, usually meat sauce (gravy)

Manicotti
Cannelloni pasta (large tubular shape) or crespelle (Italian crepes rolled into a tubular shape), with ricotta cheese filling, covered with tomato sauce and baked in a casserole

Gnocchi con Pesto
Potato dumplings with pesto sauce made from basil leaves, garlic, and pine nuts crushed together with olive oil and Parmesan cheese, from Genoa

Gnocchi con Gorgonzola
Potato dumplings with a sauce made from cream, butter, and Gorgonzola cheese (Italian blue cheese)

Bucatini all'Amatriciana
Thick spaghetti with a tomato and guanciale (Italian bacon from the cheek of the pig) sauce, from the town of Amatrice, near Rome

Risotto alla Milanese
Italian starchy, short grain (Arborio) rice cooked slowly to become creamy and flavored with saffron, from Milan

Risi e Bisi
Italian starchy, short grain (Arborio) rice cooked slowly to become creamy with peas, from Venice

Vocabulary
Cooking Methods, Meats, Fish and Shellfish

fritto	fried
bollito	boiled
arrostito	roasted
brasato / stufato	braised / stewed
affumicato	smoked
ripieno	stuffed
al forno	baked (lit. from the oven)
alla brace	broiled
alla griglia / ai ferri	grilled
alla cacciatora	stewed in a pot
cotto a puntino	cooked just right
la costoletta	chop / rib (bone in meat)
la cotoletta	cutlet (meat without bone)
la scaloppina	very thin cutlet
il pollo	chicken
il vitello	veal
i calamari	squid
i gamberi	shrimp
gli scampi	large, shrimp-like crustacean
il merluzzo	fresh cod
il baccalà	dried cod
il branzino	sea bass